SLOW COOKER
RECIPES

*A Practical and Quick Way to Cook
and Optimize Your Time*

JULY STORMS

Table of Contents

Sommario

Introduction

What is Slow Cooker

The Slow Cooker may be a special electric pot for cooking at low temperatures. In other words, once you cook with the Slow Cooker, the interior temperature will never reach 100 degrees, i.e. the boiling point, but will always remain a touch lower. How low, you'll decide to support three simple buttons on the pan (sometimes two): low, high, medium.

Since it's a low-temperature cooking process, obviously the time is going to be much longer. I've cooked stews with the Slow Cooker that went on for up to 6-10 hours. And this introduces you to the opposite button on the cooker: the time button, where you'll set the cooking time. the opposite button is that the on/off button.

It is an electrical pot with a couple of buttons to operate: time, temperature, and ignition. it's a ceramic body that's heated and a lid to retain moisture and warmth. It is often washed within the dishwasher and consumes little.

Advantages and drawbacks

The advantages are that the food doesn't burn, remains very soft and you'll also prepare sauces, soups, braised meats, stews. Dishes become nice and juicy and soft, and in particular, once you've got put all the ingredients within the pot, all you've got to try to do is press the facility button and, in quotes, "forget about" what's cooking until it is time to eat. that is what I usually do, I put the ingredients within the morning when I start working. At lunchtime I find my stew or soup nice and prepared or, if I prefer dinnertime, I even have it reheated with the buffet option, which keeps it at the perfect temperature once it's cooked. The philosophy behind this pot is ancient albeit the technology is modern the concept is that of the traditional pot placed over the stove to heat. The "pot 2.0" within the modern Slow Cooker consists of a ceramic container with a base that heats electrically.

As far as consumption cares, you'll check for yourself by consulting the booklet of a slow cooker during a store: keeping one among these devices on for a day consumes but an LED bulb. In short, slow cooking doesn't consume the maximum amount of energy.

If there's a downside to the Slow Cooker it's the dimensions. confine mind that the pots for this sort of cooking are large are composed of three parts or the part that heats the lid and therefore the ceramic container where we put the food but take up enough space. They occupy it, but I might wish to say that they also decorate it. they're aesthetically pleasing to the attention. But if space is tight it might be a drag. there's to mention that the slow cooker leaves it there: remove at the most only the ceramic container to scrub it and therefore the lid, on the other hand, the device once you've got found its place you'll always leave it there.

Where to shop for it and the way to settle on it

Also, confine in mind that if there are many of you within the family you'd better choose the larger ones so you'll make larger portions. But a 3.5 liter Slow Cooker will easily feed a family of three or four. The historical brand of Slow Cooker is that Crock-Pot, the foremost famous among the slow cookers. However, even on the market, you'll find them on the main online platforms at really honest prices, between 70 and 100 dollars. In short, different brands, in appliance stores or online

So how does the Slow Cooker work?

You choose the cooking mode that always offers a minimum of two options (low and high, and sometimes there's also an intermediate temperature), you decide on the cooking time and begin. The food should be covered with its lid, and while you are doing something else, your meat, fish, or soup will cook. most models now even have a buffet or warm function that permits you to stay your dish warm even after it's finished cooking and until you bring it to the table.

In this book, you will find many recipes for your Slow Cooker and you will soon realize that you simply won't be ready to do without it due to the big convenience you will have in cooking this manner. Enjoy!

Breakfast

Poppy Seeds Buns

Yield: 8 servings | **Prep time:** 20 minutes | **Cook time:** 5 hours

Ingredients:
3 tablespoon poppy seeds
1 teaspoon baking powder
1 egg, beaten
6 oz cottage cheese
1 cup flour
1 teaspoon ground cardamom
2 tablespoons olive oil

Directions:
Mix poppy seeds with baking powder, egg, cottage cheese, flour, and ground cardamom.
Knead the homogenous dough.
Add olive oil and keep kneading the dough for 4 minutes more.
After this, make the small buns from the dough and put them in the slow cooker bowl.
Close the lid and cook them on High for 5 hours.

Per Serving:
133 calories, 5.9g protein, 14g carbohydrates, 6.1g fat, 0.8g fiber, 22mg cholesterol, 96mg sodium, 134mg potassium.

Raspberry Chia Pudding

Yield: 2 servings | **Prep time:** 10 minutes | **Cook time:** 2 hours

Ingredients:
4 tablespoons chia seeds
1 cup of coconut milk
2 teaspoons raspberries

Directions:
Put chia seeds and coconut milk in the slow cooker and cook it for 2 hours on Low.
Then transfer the cooked chia pudding in the glasses and top with raspberries.

Per Serving:
423 calories, 7.7g protein, 19.6g carbohydrates, 37.9g fat, 13.1g fiber, 0mg cholesterol, 23mg sodium, 442mg potassium.

Shrimp Omelet

Yield: 4 servings | **Prep time:** 8 minutes | **Cook time:** 3.5 hours

Ingredients:
4 eggs, beaten
4 oz shrimps, peeled
½ teaspoon ground turmeric
½ teaspoon ground paprika
¼ teaspoon salt
Cooking spray

Directions:
Mix eggs with shrimps, turmeric, salt, and paprika.
Then spray the slow cooker bowl with cooking spray.
After this, pour the egg mixture inside. Flatten the shrimps and close the lid.
Cook the omelet for 3.5 hours on High.

Per Serving:
98 calories, 12.1g protein, 1.1g carbohydrates, 4.9g fat, 0.2g fiber, 223mg cholesterol, 278mg sodium, 120mg potassium.

Light Egg Scramble

Yield: 2 servings | **Prep time:** 15 minutes | **Cook time:** 4 hours

Ingredients:
1 tablespoon butter, melted
6 eggs, beaten
1 teaspoon salt
1 teaspoon ground paprika

Directions:
Pour the melted butter in the slow cooker.
Add eggs and salt and stir.
Cook the eggs on Low for 4 hours. Stir the eggs every 15 minutes.
When the egg scramble is cooked, top it with ground paprika.

Per Serving:
243 calories, 16.8g protein, 1.6g carbohydrates, 19g fat, 0.4g fiber, 506mg cholesterol, 1389mg sodium, 203mg potassium

Smoked Salmon Omelet

Yield: 4 servings | **Prep time:** 10 minutes | **Cook time:** 2 hours

Ingredients:
4 oz smoked salmon, sliced

5 eggs, beaten

1 teaspoon ground coriander

1 teaspoon butter, melted

Directions:
Brush the slow cooker bottom with melted butter.

Then mix eggs with ground coriander and pour the liquid in the slow cooker.

Add smoked salmon and close the lid.

Cook the omelet on High for 2 hours.

Per Serving:
120 calories, 12.1g protein, 0.4g carbohydrates, 7.7g fat, 0g fiber, 214mg cholesterol, 651mg sodium, 124mg potassium

Radish Bowl

Yield: 4 servings | **Prep time:** 10 minutes | **Cook time:** 1.5 hours

Ingredients:
2 cups radish, halved
1 tablespoon dried dill
1 tablespoon olive oil
4 eggs, beaten
¼ teaspoon salt
¼ cup milk

Directions:
Mix radish with dried dill, olive oil, salt, and milk and transfer in the slow cooker.
Cook the radish on High for 30 minutes.
Then shake the vegetables well and add eggs. Mix the mixture gently and close the lid.
Cook the meal on High for 1 hour.

Per Serving:
112 calories, 6.6g protein, 3.5g carbohydrates, 8.3g fat, 1g fiber, 165mg cholesterol, 240mg sodium, 229mg potassium

Olive Eggs

Yield: 4 servings | **Prep time:** 10 minutes | **Cook time:** 2 hours

Ingredients:
10 kalamata olives, sliced

8 eggs, beaten

1 teaspoon cayenne pepper

1 tablespoon butter

Directions:
Grease the slow cooker bottom with butter.

Then add beaten eggs and cayenne pepper.

After this, top the eggs with olives and close the lid.

Cook the eggs on High for 2 hours.

Per Serving:
165 calories, 11.2g protein, 1.6g carbohydrates, 12.9g fat, 0.5g fiber, 335mg cholesterol, 240mg sodium, 129mg potassium

Bacon Eggs

Yield: 2 servings | **Prep time:** 10 minutes | **Cook time:** 2 hours

Ingredients:
2 bacon slices
2 eggs, hard-boiled, peeled
¼ teaspoon ground black pepper
1 teaspoon olive oil
½ teaspoon dried thyme

Directions:
Sprinkle the bacon with ground black pepper and dried thyme.
Then wrap the eggs in the bacon and sprinkle with olive oil.
Put the eggs in the slow cooker and cook on High for 2 hours.

Per Serving:
187 calories, 12.6g protein, 0.9g carbohydrates, 14.7g fat, 0.2g fiber,
185mg cholesterol, 501mg sodium, 172mg potassium.

Basil Sausages

Yield: 5 servings | **Prep time:** 10 minutes | **Cook time:** 4 hours

Ingredients:
1-pound Italian sausages, chopped
1 teaspoon dried basil
1 tablespoon olive oil
1 teaspoon ground coriander
¼ cup of water

Directions:
Sprinkle the chopped sausages with ground coriander and dried basil and transfer in the slow cooker.
Add olive oil and water.
Close the lid and cook the sausages on high for 4 hours.

Per Serving:
338 calories, 12.9g protein, 0.6g carbohydrates, 31.2g fat, 0g fiber, 69mg cholesterol, 664mg sodium, 231mg potassium.

Soups, Chilies & Stews

Snow Peas Soup

Yield: 4 servings | **Prep time:** 10 minutes | **Cook time:** 3.5 hours

Ingredients:
1 tablespoon chives, chopped
1 teaspoon ground ginger
8 oz salmon fillet, chopped
5 oz bamboo shoots, canned, chopped
2 cups snow peas
1 teaspoon hot sauce
5 cups of water

Directions:
Put bamboo shoots in the slow cooker.
Add ground ginger, salmon, snow peas, and water.
Close the lid and cook the soup for 3 hours on high.
Then add hot sauce and chives. Stir the soup carefully and cook for 30 minutes on high.

Per Serving:
120 calories, 14.6g protein, 7.9g carbohydrates, 3.8g fat, 3.1g fiber, 25mg cholesterol, 70mg sodium, 612mg potassium

Beef Liver Stew

Yield: 3 servings | **Prep time:** 15 minutes | **Cook time:** 7 hours

Ingredients:
6 oz beef liver, cut into strips
2 tablespoons all-purpose flour
1 tablespoon olive oil
½ cup sour cream
½ cup of water
1 onion, roughly chopped
1 teaspoon ground black pepper

Directions:
Mix beef liver with flour and roast it in the olive oil on high heat for 2 minutes per side.
Then transfer the liver in the slow cooker.
Add all remaining ingredients and close the lid.
Cook the stew on low for 7 hours.

Per Serving:
257 calories, 17.3g protein, 12.4g carbohydrates, 15.5g fat, 1.1g fiber, 233mg cholesterol, 67mg sodium, 323mg potassium.

Mexican Style Stew

Yield: 6 servings | **Prep time:** 10 minutes | **Cook time:** 6 hours

Ingredients:
1 cup corn kernels
1 cup green peas
¼ cup white rice
4 cups chicken stock
1 teaspoon taco seasoning
1 teaspoon dried cilantro
1 tablespoon butter

Directions:
Put butter and wild rice in the slow cooker.
Then add corn kernels, green peas, chicken stock, taco seasoning, and dried cilantro.
Close the lid and cook the stew on Low for 6 hours.

Per Serving:
97 calories, 3.2g protein, 15.6g carbohydrates, 2.7g fat, 2g fiber, 5mg cholesterol, 599mg sodium, 148mg potassium.

Beans Stew

Yield: 3 servings | **Prep time:** 10 minutes | **Cook time:** 5 hours

Ingredients:
½ cup sweet pepper, chopped
¼ cup onion, chopped
1 cup edamame beans
1 cup tomatoes
1 teaspoon cayenne pepper
5 cups of water
2 tablespoons cream cheese

Directions:
Mix water with cream cheese and pour the liquid in the slow cooker.
Add cayenne pepper, edamame beans, and onion.
Then chop the tomatoes roughly and add in the slow cooker.
Close the lid and cook the stew on high for 5 hours.

Per Serving:
74 calories, 3.4g protein, 7.9g carbohydrates, 3.6g fat, 2.4g fiber, 7mg cholesterol, 109mg sodium, 218mg potassium.

Rice, Grains & Beans

Dumplings with Polenta

Yield: 6 servings | **Prep time:** 20 minutes | **Cook time:** 45 minutes

Ingredients:
3 oz polenta

3 oz flour

2 oz Cheddar cheese, shredded

½ cup of coconut milk

1 egg, beaten

3 oz water, hot

Directions:
Mix polenta and flour. Add egg and coconut milk. Mix the ingredients well.

Add cheddar cheese and knead the soft dough.

Cut the dough into 6 pieces and roll them into balls.

Pour water in the slow cooker.

Add polenta balls and cook them for 45 minutes on HIGH.

Drain the water and transfer the dumplings in the serving plates.

Per Serving:
198 calories,6.3g protein, 23.5g carbohydrates, 8.9g fat, 1.2g fiber, 37mg cholesterol, 73mg sodium, 87mg potassium.

Chicken Dip

Yield: 4 servings | **Prep time:** 10 minutes | **Cook time:** 3.5 hours

Ingredients:
½ cup white beans, canned, drained
½ cup ground chicken
1 teaspoon dried parsley
¼ cup BBQ sauce
1 teaspoon cayenne pepper
½ cup of water

Directions:
Blend the canned beans and transfer them in the slow cooker.
Add ground chicken, dried parsley, BBQ sauce, cayenne pepper, and water.
Stir the ingredients and close the lid.
Cook the dip on High for 3.5 hours.

Per Serving:
142 calories, 11g protein, 21.2g carbohydrates, 1.6g fat, 4.1g fiber, 16mg cholesterol, 195mg sodium, 539mg potassium.

Pasta Fritters

Yield: 4 servings | **Prep time:** 15 minutes | **Cook time:** 5 hours

Ingredients:
7 oz whole-grain pasta, cooked

1 egg, beaten

½ cup Cheddar cheese

1 teaspoon ground turmeric

1 tablespoon whole-grain flour

1 teaspoon sesame oil

Directions:
Chop the pasta into small pieces and mix with egg, ground turmeric, and flour.

Then shred the cheese and add it in the pasta mixture.

Make the small fritters from the mixture.

After this, brush the slow cooker bowl with sesame oil.

Put the fritters inside and cook them on low for 5 hours.

Per Serving:
144 calories, 7g protein, 12.4g carbohydrates, 7.4g fat, 1.6g fiber, 56mg cholesterol, 103mg sodium, 103g potassium.

Spiced Bulgur

Yield: 3 servings | **Prep time:** 15 minutes | **Cook time:** 6 hours

Ingredients:
1 cup bulgur
1.5 cup chicken stock
½ cup of water
½ teaspoon cayenne pepper
½ teaspoon ground nutmeg
½ teaspoon ground cardamom
1 tablespoon coconut oil

Directions:
Melt the coconut oil in the skillet, add bulgur and roast for 2-3 minutes on high heat.
'Then transfer the bulgur in the slow cooker.
Add chicken stock and all remaining ingredients.
Close the lid and cook the meal on low for 6 hours.

Per Serving:
207 calories, 6.2g protein, 36.4g carbohydrates, 5.6g fat, 8.8g fiber, 0mg cholesterol, 390mg sodium, 210mg potassium.

Poultry

Bourbon Chicken Cubes

Yield: 4 servings | **Prep time:** 10 minutes | **Cook time:** 4 hours

Ingredients:
½ cup bourbon
1 teaspoon liquid honey
1 tablespoon BBQ sauce
1 white onion, diced
1 teaspoon garlic powder
1-pound chicken fillet, cubed

Directions:
Put all ingredients in the slow cooker.
Mix the mixture until liquid honey is dissolved.
Then close the lid and cook the meal on high for 4 hours.

Per Serving:
304 calories, 33.2g protein, 5.9g carbohydrates, 8.5g fat, 0.7g fiber, 101mg cholesterol, 143mg sodium, 333mg potassium.

Pineapple Chicken

Yield: 4 servings | **Prep time:** 15 minutes | **Cook time:** 8 hours

Ingredients:
12 oz chicken fillet
1 cup pineapple, canned, chopped
½ cup Cheddar cheese, shredded
1 tablespoon butter, softened
1 teaspoon ground black pepper
¼ cup of water

Directions:
Grease the slow cooker bowl bottom with softened butter.
Then cut the chicken fillet into servings and put in the slow cooker in one layer.
After this, top the chicken with ground black pepper, water, pineapple, and Cheddar cheese.
Close the lid and cook the meal on Low for 8 hours.

Per Serving:
266 calories, 28.4g protein, 5.9g carbohydrates, 13.9g fat, 0.7g fiber, 98mg cholesterol, 183mg sodium, 273mg potassium.

Greece Style Chicken

Yield: 6 servings | **Prep time:** 10 minutes | 12 oz chicken fillet, chopped
1 cup green olives, chopped
1 cup of water
1 tablespoon cream cheese
½ teaspoon dried thyme

Directions:
Put all ingredients in the slow cooker.
Close the lid and cook the meal on Low for 8 hours.
Then transfer the cooked chicken in the bowls and top with olives and hot liquid from the slow cooker.

Per Serving:
124 calories,16.7g protein, 0.8g carbohydrates, 5.7g fat, 0.3g fiber, 52mg cholesterol, 167mg sodium, 142mg potassium.

Garlic Pulled Chicken

Yield: 4 servings | **Prep time:** 10 minutes | **Cook time:** 4 hours

Ingredients:
1-pound chicken breast, skinless, boneless
1 tablespoon minced garlic
2 cups of water
½ cup plain yogurt

Directions:
Put the chicken breast in the slow cooker.
Add minced garlic and water.
Close the lid and cook the chicken on High for 4 hours.
Then drain water and shred the chicken breast.
Add plain yogurt and stir the pulled chicken well.

Per Serving:
154 calories, 25.9g protein, 2.9g carbohydrates, 3.2g fat, 0g fiber, 74mg cholesterol, 83mg sodium, 501mg potassium.

Salsa Chicken Wings

Yield: 5 servings | **Prep time:** 10 minutes | **Cook time:** 6 hours

Ingredients:
2-pounds chicken wings
2 cups salsa
½ cup of water

Directions:
Put all ingredients in the slow cooker.
Carefully mix the mixture and close the lid.
Cook the chicken wings on low for 6 hours.

Per Serving:
373 calories, 54.1g protein, 6.5g carbohydrates, 13.6g fat, 1.7g fiber,
161mg cholesterol, 781mg sodium, 750mg potassium.

Ground Turkey Bowl

Yield: 4 servings | **Prep time:** 10 minutes | **Cook time:** 2.5 hours

Ingredients:
2 tomatoes, chopped
10 oz ground turkey
1 cup Monterey Jack cheese, shredded
½ cup cream
1 teaspoon ground black pepper

Directions:
Put ground turkey in the slow cooker.
Add cheese, cream, and ground black pepper.
Close the lid and cook the meal on High for 2.5 hours.
Then carefully mix the mixture and transfer in the serving bowls.
Top the ground turkey with chopped tomatoes.

Per Serving:
275 calories, 27.2g protein, 3.9g carbohydrates, 18.1g fat, 0.9g fiber, 103mg cholesterol, 240mg sodium, 378mg potassium.

Stuffed Chicken Fillets

Yield: 6 servings | **Prep time:** 20 minutes | **Cook time:** 4 hours

Ingredients:
½ cup green peas, cooked
½ cup long-grain rice, cooked
16 oz chicken fillets
1 cup of water
1 teaspoon Italian seasonings

Directions:
Make the horizontal cuts in chicken fillets.
After this, mix Italian seasonings with rice and green peas.
Fill the chicken fillet with rice mixture and secure them with toothpicks.
Put the chicken fillets in the slow cooker.
Add water and close the lid.
Cook the chicken on high for 4 hours.

Per Serving:
212 calories, 23.6g protein, 14.2g carbohydrates, 6g fat, 0.8g fiber, 68mg cholesterol, 68mg sodium, 232mg potassium.

Beef

Beef Roast

Yield: 5 servings | **Prep time:** 10 minutes | **Cook time:** 6 hours

Ingredients:
1-pound beef chuck roast
1 tablespoon ketchup
1 tablespoon mayonnaise
1 teaspoon chili powder
1 teaspoon olive oil
1 teaspoon lemon juice
½ cup of water

Directions:
In the bowl mix ketchup, mayonnaise, chili powder, olive oil, and lemon juice.
Then sprinkle the beef chuck roast with ketchup mixture.
Pour the water in the slow cooker.
Add beef chuck roast and close the lid.
Cook the meat on High for 6 hours.

Per Serving:
354 calories, 23.9g protein, 1.8g carbohydrates, 27.3g fat, 0.2g fiber, 94mg cholesterol, 119mg sodium, 230mg potassium.

Beef Brisket in Orange Juice

Yield: 4 servings | **Prep time:** 15 minutes | **Cook time:** 5 hours

Ingredients:
1 cup of orange juice
2 cups of water
2 tablespoons butter
12 oz beef brisket
½ teaspoon salt

Directions:
Toss butter in the skillet and melt.
Put the beef brisket in the melted butter and roast on high heat for 3 minutes per side.
Then sprinkle the meat with salt and transfer in the slow cooker.
Add orange juice and water.
Close the lid and cook the meat on High for 5 hours.

Per Serving:
237 calories, 26.3g protein, 6.5g carbohydrates, 11.2g fat, 0.1g fiber, 91mg cholesterol, 392mg sodium, 470mg potassium.

Beef Bolognese

Yield: 4 servings | **Prep time:** 15 minutes | **Cook time:** 5 hours

Ingredients:
½ cup onion, diced

1 teaspoon dried basil

1 teaspoon dried cilantro

½ cup tomato juice

1 tablespoon sesame oil

1-pound ground beef

2 oz parmesan, grated

Directions:
In the mixing bowl mix ground beef with cilantro, basil, and onion.

Pour the sesame oil in the slow cooker.

Add tomato juice and ground beef mixture.

Cook it on high for 3 hours.

Then add parmesan and carefully mix.

Cook the meal on low for 2 hours more.

Per Serving:
297 calories, 39.4g protein, 3.2g carbohydrates, 13.5g fat, 0.4g fiber, 111mg cholesterol, 289mg sodium, 548mg potassium.

Pickled Pulled Beef

Yield: 4 servings | **Prep time:** 10 minutes | **Cook time:** 5 hours

Ingredients:
1 cup cucumber pickles, chopped
10 oz beef sirloin
1 teaspoon ground black pepper
1 teaspoon salt
2 cups of water
2 tablespoons mayonnaise

Directions:
Pour water in the slow cooker.
Add beef sirloin, ground black pepper, and salt.
Close the lid and cook the beef on high for 5 hours.
Then drain water and chop the beef.
Put the beef in the big bowl.
Add chopped cucumber pickles and mayonnaise.
Mix the beef well.

Per Serving:
162 calories, 21.6g protein, 2.1g carbohydrates, 6.9g fat, 0.1g fiber, 65mg cholesterol, 719mg sodium, 294mg potassium.

Barbacoa Beef

Yield: 4 servings | **Prep time:** 20 minutes | **Cook time:** 5 hours

Ingredients:
1-pound beef chuck roast
1 teaspoon ground black pepper
½ teaspoon salt
1 teaspoon ground cumin
¼ lime,
½ teaspoon ground clove
2 cups of water

Directions:
Put the beef in the slow cooker.
Add ground black pepper, salt, ground cumin, ground clove, and water.
Close the lid and cook the meat on High for 5 hours.
Then shred the beef.
Squeeze the line over the meat and carefully mix.

Per Serving:
417 calories, 29.9g protein, 1.2g carbohydrates, 31.8g fat, 0.4g fiber,
117mg cholesterol, 369mg sodium, 283mg potassium.

Delightful Pepperoncini Beef

Yield: 4 servings | **Prep time:** 10 minutes | **Cook time:** 5 hours

Ingredients:
2 oz pepperoncini
1-pound beef chuck roast
2 cups of water
1 teaspoon minced garlic

Directions:
Chop the beef roughly and mix with minced garlic.
Then transfer the beef in the slow cooker.
Add water and pepperoncini.
Close the lid and cook the meal on High for 5 hours.

Per Serving:
418 calories, 29.9g protein, 1.7g carbohydrates, 31.6g fat, 0g fiber,
117mg cholesterol, 216mg sodium, 263mg potassium.

Beef Meatloaf

Yield: 6 servings | **Prep time:** 15 minutes | **Cook time:** 6 hours

Ingredients:
1-pound ground beef
1 cup celery stalk, diced
3 tablespoons semolina
1 teaspoon garlic, diced
1 teaspoon cayenne pepper
1 tablespoon coconut oil, softened
1 teaspoon salt
½ cup Monterey Jack cheese, shredded

Directions:
In the mixing bowl mix ground beef with a celery stalk, semolina, garlic, cayenne pepper, and salt.
Then grease the slow cooker bottom with coconut oil.
Put the ground beef mixture and flatten it.
Top the beef with Monterey jack cheese and close the lid.
Cook the meatloaf on Low for 6 hours.

Per Serving:
218 calories, 26.1g protein, 4.7g carbohydrates, 10g fat, 0.6g fiber, 76mg cholesterol, 502mg sodium, 374mg potassium.

Pork&Lamb

Meat and Mushrooms Saute

Yield: 4 servings | **Prep time:** 10 minutes | **Cook time:** 5 hours

Ingredients:
8 oz pork sirloin, sliced
1 cup white mushrooms, chopped
1 onion, sliced
1 cup cream
1 teaspoon ground black pepper
1 teaspoon salt

Directions:
Put all ingredients in the slow cooker and carefully mix with the help of the spatula.
Then close the lid and cook the saute on High for 5 hours.

Per Serving:
156 calories, 13g protein, 5.4g carbohydrates, 9g fat, 0.9g fiber, 47mg cholesterol, 634mg sodium, 125mg potassium

Braised Ham

Yield: 4 servings | **Prep time:** 10 minutes | **Cook time:** 10 hours

Ingredients:
12 oz smoked shoulder ham
1 tablespoon mustard
2 cups of water
¼ cup maple syrup
¼ cup beer

Directions:
Rub the smoked shoulder ham with mustard and transfer in the slow cooker.
Add water and beer.
Close the lid and cook the ham on low for 10 hours.
When the time is finished, sprinkle the meat with maple syrup and slice.

Per Serving:
221 calories, 15.7g protein, 15.7g carbohydrates, 9.9g fat, 0.4g fiber, 50mg cholesterol, 747mg sodium, 64mg potassium

Cumin Pork

Yield: 6 servings | **Prep time:** 10 minutes | **Cook time:** 5 hours

Ingredients:
1-pound pork shoulder, chopped
1 teaspoon cumin seeds
1 teaspoon garlic powder
1 teaspoon ground nutmeg
1 carrot, diced
2 cup of water
1 teaspoon salt

Directions:
Roast the cumin seeds in the skillet for 2-3 minutes or until the seeds start to smell.
Then place them in the slow cooker.
Add all remaining ingredients and close the lid.
Cook the pork on high for 5 hours.

Per Serving:
230 calories, 17.8g protein, 1.7g carbohydrates, 16.4g fat, 0.4g fiber, 68mg cholesterol, 449mg sodium, 295mg potassium

Cocoa Pork Chops

Yield: 4 servings | **Prep time:** 10 minutes | **Cook time:** 2.5 hours

Ingredients:
4 pork chops
1 tablespoon cocoa powder
½ cup cream
1 tablespoon butter
1 teaspoon ground black pepper
½ teaspoon salt
¼ cup of water

Directions:
Beat the pork chops gently with the help of the kitchen hammer.
Then sprinkle the meat with ground black pepper and salt. Transfer it
in the slow cooker.
After this, mix water with cocoa powder and cream and pour it in the
slow cooker.
Add butter and close the lid.
Cook the pork chops on high for 2.5 hours.

Per Serving:
305 calories, 18.6g protein, 2g carbohydrates, 24.6g fat, 0.5g fiber,
82mg cholesterol, 378mg sodium, 328mg potassium

Fish&Seafood

Cod Sticks

Yield: 2 servings | **Prep time:** 15 minutes | 1.5 hour

Ingredients:
2 cod fillets
1 teaspoon ground black pepper
1 egg, beaten
1/3 cup breadcrumbs
1 tablespoon coconut oil
¼ cup of water

Directions:
Cut the cod fillets into medium sticks and sprinkle with ground black pepper.
Then dip the fish in the beaten egg and coat in the breadcrumbs.
Pour water in the slow cooker.
Add coconut oil and fish sticks.
Cook the meal on High for 1.5 hours.

Per Serving:
254 calories, 25.3g protein, 13.8g carbohydrates, 11g fat, 1.1g fiber, 137mg cholesterol, 234mg sodium, 78mg potassium.

Butter Crab

Yield: 4 servings | **Prep time:** 10 minutes | **Cook time:** 4.5 hours

Ingredients:
1-pound crab meat, roughly chopped
1 tablespoon fresh parsley, chopped
3 tablespoons butter
2 tablespoons water

Directions:
Melt butter and pour it in the slow cooker.
Add water, parsley, and crab meat.
Cook the meal on Low for 4.5 hours.

Per Serving:
178 calories, 14.3g protein, 2.1g carbohydrates, 10.7g fat, 0g fiber, 84mg cholesterol, 771mg sodium, 8mg potassium.

Cilantro Haddock

Yield: 2 servings | **Prep time:** 10 minutes | **Cook time:** 1.5 hour

Ingredients:
6 oz haddock fillet
1 teaspoon dried cilantro
1 teaspoon olive oil
1 teaspoon lemon juice
¼ cup fish stock

Directions:
Heat the olive oil in the skillet well.
Then put the haddock fillet and roast it for 1 minute per side.
Transfer the fillets in the slow cooker.
Add fish stock, cilantro, and lemon juice.
Cook the fish on high for 1.5 hours.

Per Serving:
121 calories, 21.3g protein, 0.1g carbohydrates, 3.4g fat, 0g fiber, 63mg cholesterol, 120mg sodium, 385mg potassium

Mussels and Vegetable Ragout

Yield: 4 servings | **Prep time:** 10 minutes | **Cook time:** 5 hours

Ingredients:
1 cup potato, chopped
½ onion, chopped
2 cups of water
1 bell pepper, chopped
1 teaspoon peppercorns
1 cup tomatoes, chopped
1 cup mussels
1 teaspoon salt

Directions:
Put all ingredients except mussels in the slow cooker.
Close the lid and cook the meal on High for 3 hours.
Then add mussels and mix the meal.
Close the lid and cook the ragout on Low for 2 hours.

Per Serving:
71 calories, 5.8g protein, 10.3g carbohydrates, 1.1g fat, 1.8g fiber, 11mg cholesterol, 697mg sodium, 390mg potassium

Tomato Fish Casserole

Yield: 2 servings | **Prep time:** 10 minutes | **Cook time:** 6 hours

Ingredients:
2 cod fillets
½ cup tomato juice
1 cup bell pepper, chopped
1 teaspoon ground cumin
½ teaspoon salt
1 teaspoon olive oil
½ cup spinach, chopped

Directions:
Slice the cod fillets and sprinkle them with olive oil, salt, and ground cumin.
Put the fish in the slow cooker.
Top it with bell pepper and spinach.
Then add tomato juice and close the lid.
Cook the casserole on Low for 6 hours.

Per Serving:
145 calories, 21.5g protein, 7.8g carbohydrates, 3.8g fat, 1.3g fiber, 55mg cholesterol, 824mg sodium, 312mg potassium

Creamy Onion Casserole

Yield: 6 servings | **Prep time:** 10 minutes | **Cook time:** 3 hours

Ingredients:
3 white onions, sliced
1 cup cream
1-pound salmon fillet, chopped
1 teaspoon ground coriander
¼ cup fresh parsley, chopped
2 tablespoons breadcrumbs

Directions:
Sprinkle the salmon fillet with ground coriander and coat in the breadcrumbs.
Put the fish in the slow cooker.
Then top it with sliced onion and fresh parsley.
Add cream and close the lid.
Cook the casserole on High for 3 hours.

Per Serving:
158 calories, 16g protein, 8.2g carbohydrates, 7.1g fat, 1.4g fiber, 41mg cholesterol, 66mg sodium, 404mg potassium

Fish Soufflé

Yield: 4 servings | **Prep time:** 10 minutes | **Cook time:** 7 hours

Ingredients:
4 eggs, beaten
8 oz salmon fillet, chopped
¼ cup of coconut milk
2 oz Provolone cheese, grated

Directions:
Mix coconut milk with eggs and pour the liquid in the slow cooker.
Add salmon and cheese.
Close the lid and cook soufflé for 7 hours on low.

Per Serving:
222 calories, 20.5g protein, 1.5g carbohydrates, 15.2g fat, 0.3g fiber, 198mg cholesterol, 212mg sodium, 336mg potassium

Vegetarian Mains

Potato Salad

Yield: 2 servings | **Prep time:** 10 minutes | **Cook time:** 3 hours

Ingredients:
1 cup potato, chopped
1 cup of water
1 teaspoon salt
2 oz celery stalk, chopped
2 oz fresh parsley, chopped
¼ onion, diced
1 tablespoon mayonnaise

Directions:
Put the potatoes in the slow cooker.
Add water and salt.
Cook the potatoes on High for 3 hours.
Then drain water and transfer the potatoes in the salad bowl.
Add all remaining ingredients and carefully mix the salad.

Per Serving:
129 calories, 5.5g protein, 12.4g carbohydrates, 6.7g fat, 2.5g fiber, 12mg cholesterol, 1479mg sodium, 465mg potassium.

Sweet Potato Puree

Yield: 2 servings | **Prep time:** 15 minutes | **Cook time:** 4 hours

Ingredients:
2 cups sweet potato, chopped
1 cup of water
¼ cup half and half
1 oz scallions, chopped
1 teaspoon salt

Directions:
Put sweet potatoes in the slow cooker.
Add water and salt.
Cook them on High for 4 hours.
The drain water and transfer the sweet potatoes in the food processor.
Add half and half and blend until smooth.
Transfer the puree in the bowl, and scallions, and mix carefully.

Per Serving:
225 calories, 5.2g protein, 43.7g carbohydrates, 3.9g fat, 7g fiber, 11mg cholesterol, 1253mg sodium, 1030mg potassium.

Hot Tofu

Yield: 4 servings | **Prep time:** 10 minutes | **Cook time:** 4 hours

Ingredients:
1-pound firm tofu, cubed
1 tablespoon hot sauce
½ cup vegetable stock
1 teaspoon miso paste

Directions:
Mix vegetables tock with miso paste and pour in the slow cooker.
Add hot sauce and tofu.
Close the lid and cook the meal on Low for 4 hours.
Then transfer the tofu and liquid in the serving bowls.

Per Serving:
83 calories, 9.5g protein, 2.5g carbohydrates, 4.8g fat, 1.2g fiber, 0mg cholesterol, 168mg sodium, 176mg potassium.

Fragrant Jackfruit

Yield: 4 servings | **Prep time:** 15 minutes | **Cook time:** 2 hours

Ingredients:
1-pound jackfruit, canned, chopped
1 teaspoon tomato paste
1 teaspoon taco seasoning
1 onion, diced
½ cup coconut cream
1 teaspoon chili powder

Directions:
In the mixing bowl mix taco seasoning, chili powder, tomato paste, and coconut cream.
Put the jackfruit and diced onion in the slow cooker.
Pour the tomato mixture over the vegetables and gently mix them.
Close the lid and cook the meal on High for 2 hours.

Per Serving:
145 calories, 2.4g protein, 32.4g carbohydrates, 2.2g fat, 2.7g fiber, 6mg cholesterol, 127mg sodium, 421mg potassium.

Tofu Curry

Yield: 4 servings | **Prep time:** 10 minutes | **Cook time:** 3 hours

Ingredients:
1 cup chickpeas, cooked
8 oz firm tofu, chopped
1 teaspoon curry powder
½ cup of coconut milk
1 teaspoon ground coriander
1 cup vegetable stock
1 red onion, diced

Directions:
In the mixing bowl mix curry powder, coconut milk, ground coriander, and red onion.
Mix the curry mixture with tofu.
Then pour the vegetable stock in the slow cooker.
Add chickpeas, tofu, and all remaining curry mixture.
Close the lid and cook the meal on Low for 3 hours. Don't stir the cooked meal.

Per Serving:
306 calories, 15.3g protein, 36.3g carbohydrates, 13.1g fat, 10.6g fiber, 0mg cholesterol, 205mg sodium, 649mg potassium.

Eggplant Casserole

Yield: 4 servings | **Prep time:** 15 minutes | **Cook time:** 6 hours

Ingredients:
1 teaspoon minced garlic

2 cups eggplants, chopped

2 tablespoons sunflower oil

1 teaspoon salt

½ cup potato, diced

1 cup of water

1 cup vegan Cheddar cheese, shredded

Directions:
Brush the slow cooker bottom with sunflower oil.

The mix eggplants with minced garlic and salt.

Put the vegetables in the slow cooker.

Add potatoes and water.

After this, top the vegetables with vegan Cheddar cheese and close the lid.

Cook the casserole on Low for 6 hours.

Per Serving:
194 calories, 7.7g protein, 4.6g carbohydrates, 16.4g fat, 1.7g fiber, 30mg cholesterol, 760mg sodium, 165mg potassium.

Corn Fritters

Yield: 4 servings | **Prep time:** 15 minutes | **Cook time:** 3 hours

Ingredients:
1 cup mashed potato
1/3 cup corn kernels, cooked
1 egg, beaten
2 tablespoons flour
1 teaspoon salt
1 teaspoon ground turmeric
½ teaspoon chili powder
2 tablespoons coconut oil

Directions:
Put the coconut oil in the slow cooker and melt it on low for 15 minutes.
Meanwhile, mix mashed potato with corn kernels, egg, flour, salt, ground turmeric, and chili powder.
Make the medium size fritters and put them in the slow cooker.
Cook them on Low for 3 hours.

Per Serving:
162 calories, 3.3g protein, 14.9g carbohydrates, 10.4g fat, 1.5g fiber, 41mg cholesterol, 777mg sodium, 246mg potassium.

Garlic Asparagus

Yield: 5 servings | **Prep time:** 10 minutes | **Cook time:** 6 hours

Ingredients:
1-pound asparagus, trimmed
1 teaspoon salt
1 teaspoon garlic powder
1 tablespoon vegan butter
1 ½ cup vegetable stock

Directions:
Chop the asparagus roughly and sprinkle with salt and garlic powder.
Put the vegetables in the slow cooker.
Add vegan butter and vegetable stock. Close the lid.
Cook the asparagus on Low for 6 hours.

Per Serving:
33 calories, 2.3g protein, 6.1g carbohydrates, 1g fat, 2g fiber, 0mg
cholesterol, 687mg sodium, 190mg potassium.

Dessert

Pear Crumble

Yield: 2 servings | **Prep time:** 10 minutes | **Cook time:** 3 hours

Ingredients:
4 tablespoons oatmeal
1 pear, chopped
2 tablespoons sugar
1 tablespoon coconut oil
½ teaspoon ground cardamom
1 tablespoon dried apricots, chopped
¼ cup of coconut milk

Directions:
Mix oatmeal with chopped pear, sugar, coconut oil, ground cardamom, dried apricots, and coconut milk.
Then put the mixture in the slow cooker and close the lid.
Cook the crumble on Low for 3 hours.

Per Serving:
255 calories, 2.4g protein, 32g carbohydrates, 14.8g fat, 4.1g fiber, 0mg cholesterol,6mg sodium, 215mg potassium.

Sweet Baked Milk

Yield: 5 servings | **Prep time:** 10 minutes | **Cook time:** 10 hours

Ingredients:
4 cups of milk
3 tablespoons sugar
½ teaspoon vanilla extract

Directions:
Mix milk with sugar and vanilla extract and stir until sugar is dissolved.
Then pour the liquid in the slow cooker and close the lid.
Cook the milk on Low for 10 hours.

Per Serving:
126 calories, 6.4g protein, 16.9g carbohydrates, 4g fat, 3g fiber, 16mg
cholesterol, 92mg sodium, 113mg potassium.

Cardamom Apple Jam

Yield: 4 servings | **Prep time:** 15 minutes | **Cook time:** 2.5 hours

Ingredients:
1 cup apples, chopped
1 teaspoon ground cardamom
2 tablespoons brown sugar
1 teaspoon agar

Directions:
Mix apples with brown sugar and transfer in the slow cooker.
Leave the apples until they get the juice.
Then add ground cardamom and agar. Mix the mixture.
Close the lid and cook the jam on High for 2.5 hours.
Then blend the mixture until smooth and cool to room temperature.

Per Serving:
48 calories, 0.2g protein, 12.5g carbohydrates, 0.1g fat, 1.5g fiber, 0mg cholesterol, 2mg sodium, 72mg potassium.

Chocolate Mango

Yield: 6 servings | **Prep time:** 10 minutes | **Cook time:** 4 hours

Ingredients:
1-pound mango, puree
2 oz milk chocolate, chopped
1 cup coconut cream

Directions:
Mix mango with coconut cream.
Then transfer the mixture in the ramekins.
Top every ramekin with chocolate and cover with foil.
Place the ramekins in the slow cooker and close the lid.
Cook the meal on Low for 4 hours.

Per Serving:
188 calories, 2.3g protein, 19.2g carbohydrates, 12.6g fat, 2.4g fiber, 2mg cholesterol, 14mg sodium, 267mg potassium.

Coconut and Lemon Pie

Yield: 6 servings | **Prep time:** 10 minutes | **Cook time:** 4.5 hours

Ingredients:
1 teaspoon baking powder
1 lemon, sliced
1 cup coconut flour
1 cup all-purpose flour
1 teaspoon vanilla extract
4 tablespoons sugar
1 cup skim milk
2 tablespoons coconut shred
Cooking spray

Directions:
Spray the slow cooker with cooking spray from inside.
Then mix skim milk with sugar, vanilla extract, all types of flour, and baking powder.
When you get a homogenous mixture, pour it in the slow cooker.
Then sprinkle the dough with sliced lemon and shredded coconut.
Close the lid and cook the pie on High for 4.5 hours.

Per Serving:
223 calories, 6.3g protein, 41.3g carbohydrates, 3.9g fat, 9.2g fiber, 1mg cholesterol, 24mg sodium, 184mg potassium.

Rhubarb Jam

Yield: 6 servings | **Prep time:** 10 minutes | **Cook time:** 8 hours

Ingredients:
2-pounds rhubarb, chopped
1 cup of sugar
1 teaspoon lime zest, grated
¼ cup of water

Directions:
Put all ingredients in the slow cooker.
Cook the jam on Low for 8 hours.
Then transfer it in the glass jars and cool well.

Per Serving:
157 calories, 1.4g protein, 40.2g carbohydrates, 0.3g fat, 2.8g fiber, 0mg cholesterol, 6mg sodium, 436mg potassium.

Sautéed Figs

Yield: 6 servings | **Prep time:** 10 minutes | **Cook time:** 2 hours

Ingredients:
6 fresh figs
2 tablespoons butter
2 tablespoons maple syrup
1 tablespoon raisins
1 cup of water

Directions:
Put butter and figs in the slow cooker.
Add raisins and water.
Close the lid and cook the meal on High for 2 hours.
Then transfer the cooked figs in the plates and sprinkle with maple syrup.

Per Serving:
103 calories, 0.7g protein, 17.8g carbohydrates, 4g fat, 1.9g fiber, 10mg cholesterol, 31mg sodium, 156mg potassium.

Prune Bake

Yield: 4 servings | **Prep time:** 15 minutes | **Cook time:** 3 hours

Ingredients:
2 cups of cottage cheese
5 eggs, beaten
1 cup prunes, chopped
4 teaspoons butter

Directions:
Mix cottage cheese with eggs and blend the mixture until smooth and fluffy.
Then put the butter into 4 ramekins.
Mix cottage cheese mixture with prunes and transfer in the ramekins with butter.
Transfer the ramekins in the slow cooker and close the lid.
Cook the meal on High for 3 hours.

Per Serving:
316 calories, 23.4g protein, 31.7g carbohydrates, 11.6g fat, 3g fiber, 224mg cholesterol, 564mg sodium, 494mg potassium.

Avocado Jelly

Yield: 2 servings | **Prep time:** 15 minutes | **Cook time:** 1.5 hours

Ingredients:
1 avocado, pitted, chopped
1 cup of orange juice
1 tablespoon gelatin
3 tablespoons brown sugar

Directions:
Pour orange juice in the slow cooker.
Add brown sugar and cook the liquid on High for 1.5 hours.
Then add gelatin and stir the mixture until smooth.
After this, blend the avocado until smooth, add orange juice liquid and mix until homogenous.
Pour it in the cups and refrigerate until solid.

Per Serving:
324 calories, 5.8g protein, 34.8g carbohydrates, 19.9g fat, 7g fiber, 0mg cholesterol, 18mg sodium, 754mg potassium.

Milky Custard

Yield: 6 servings | **Prep time:** 10 minutes | **Cook time:** 7 hours

Ingredients:
3 cups of milk
3 tablespoons corn starch
1 teaspoon ground cardamom
1 cup of sugar

Directions:
Mix sugar with ground cardamom and corn starch.
Add milk and whisk the mixture until smooth.
After this, pour the liquid in the slow cooker and cook it on Low for 7 hours. Stir the mixture every 1 hour.
Then cool the cooked custard well and transfer in the ramekins.

Per Serving:
205 calories, 4g protein, 44.1g carbohydrates, 2.5g fat, 0.1g fiber, 10mg cholesterol, 58mg sodium, 74mg potassium.

Flax Seeds Bars

Yield: 8 servings | **Prep time:** 15 minutes | **Cook time:** 4 hours

Ingredients:
1 cup flax seeds
1 cup of chocolate chips
¼ cup cream
3 oz nuts, chopped
1 tablespoon coconut oil

Directions:
Line the slow cooker bottom with baking paper.
Then put all ingredients inside and close the lid.
Cook the mixture on low for 4 hours.
Then open the lid and make the mixture homogenous.
Transfer it in the silicone mold and flatten well.
Refrigerate it until solid and crush into bars.

Per Serving:
269 calories, 6.1g protein, 19.4g carbohydrates, 18.2g fat, 5.5g fiber, 6mg cholesterol, 94mg sodium, 258mg potassium.